RUTHANN JOHNSON

Copyright ©2023 By Ruthann Johnson

All Rights Reserved. No part of this book may be used or reproduced by any means, graphic, electronic, or mechanical, including photocopying, recording, taping, or by any information storage retrieval system without the written permission of the publisher except in the case of brief quotations embodied in critical articles and reviews.

Unless otherwise identified, Scripture quotations are taken from the King James Version (KJV).

Amplified Bible (AMP)
Scripture quotations marked AMP are taken from the Amplified Bible copyright © 2015 by The Lockman Foundation, La Habra, CA 90631. All rights reserved.

Amplified Bible, Classic Edition (AMPC)
Scripture quotations marked AMPC are taken from the Amplified Bible, Classic Edition. Copyright © 1954, 1958, 1962, 1964, 1965, 1987 by The Lockman Foundation. All rights reserved.

New Living Translation (NLT)
Scripture quotations marked NLT are taken from the Holy Bible, New Living Translation, copyright © 1996, 2004, 2015 by Tyndale House Foundation. Used by permission of Tyndale House Publishers, Inc., Carol Stream, Illinois 60188. All rights reserved.

The Passion Translation (TPT)
Scripture quotations marked TPT are from The Passion Translation®. Copyright © 2017, 2018, 2020 by Passion & Fire Ministries, Inc. Used by permission. All rights reserved.

The Message (MSG).
Scripture quotations marked (MSG) are from THE MESSAGE: The Bible in Contemporary Language copyright © 1993, 2002, 2018 by Eugene H. Peterson. All rights reserved. Used by permission of NavPress. Represented by Tyndale House Publishers.

Foreword

I am so grateful to God that I met Ruthann Johnson, the author of this great book. This book is undoubtedly a testament of her life as I have witnessed it for myself. I will be the first to get a copy and put it on the top shelf in my library because of the lessons I've learned from her life. Sometimes we don't know how much our lives impact others and Ruthann's story has impacted mine greatly, as it will impact yours.

Today I see a transformed woman of God and a daughter in Christ I am very proud of. She withstood the test of time that built her character and now she can return to empower others. I am thankful God connected us when He did. You are an amazing person Ruthann, and I know your pleasant heart will be on display and will help others through critical transitions in life. God Bless you and may life continue to extend its best for you.

With much love.
Pastor Dr. Lincoln Coffie (D. Div.)
Emergency Medicine Physician (ABEM)

Dedication

Before, you were just my First Lady, then you became my mother (spiritually). I didn't know how much I needed you until I returned like the prodigal son returned to his father. I still remember your counsel before I entered what I consider the wilderness season of my life. You were my confidant, my personal intercessor; even when my heart shifted, I could still hear you calling me from a distance. And when I returned, you gave me your best to ensure that I was restored.

Then there was the one you assigned to me; my friend, who spoke life into me. I sit here trying to find the right words to explain the magnitude of the impact you've both had on my life. To the woman you assigned to me; who stayed with me in the hospital when I got sick in the beginning of that season. I didn't know that three years later you'd be the one to nurse the wounds and help me regain my true identity. I honor you and I am grateful for you. Thank you for every prayer, lesson, correction and instruction.

I dedicate this book to the two women whose lives have been my example. The women who taught me the true Art of Transiting. Like a midwife and a nurse, you labored with me and this book is my firstborn.

To my spiritual mother, Pastor Dr. Apryl Coffie; and to the one you assigned to me; Minister Titania Clark; I love you both dearly, thank you.

Acknowledgement

It's not the thing you do, to just to get it out the way, it's the thing you do because you understand that God in his sovereignty, loved you enough to position you at the right place and surround you with the right people. For this reason, I want to pause to acknowledge the people who without them, I would not be here:

- To my mother; Monica Johnson, the Lord orders my steps and you have continued to watch and pray over them.

- To my Dad, Linford Johnson; my constant example of endurance, humility and strength.

- To my spiritual parents, Pastors Dr. Lincoln and Dr. Apryl Coffie, my life has forever changed because of your sacrifice, your belief in me and your constant support.

- To my brothers: Pastor Phillip Johnson, I wouldn't be here if it wasn't for you going before me and making the way for me. Peter and Junior Johnson; you have always been my company and my encouragers, thank you.

- To the women who helped me along the way, Minister Deavonne Johnson, Apostle Elizabeth Roberts, Tracy-Ann Johnson and Jenny Johnson; for praying for me when I was too wounded to pray for myself, for being my confidants, for covering me until I recovered, for taking a chance on me, for believing in me. Thank you.

- To the Israel family, thank you for taking a chance on me and for providing an environment for me to learn and grow. As challenging as that season was, the office was the one place I looked forward to going to every week and to the rest of my coworkers in Illinois, thank you.

- To Apostle Louis Wimbley and Prophetess Shanea Wimbley and the rest of the Manifest Chicago family, the Refresh Team, Prophetess Makiyah Jones and Prophet Laron Matthews, thank you for every kind gesture, every word of encouragement and for every prayer.

- Lastly, to the head of my life; Jesus, my Lord and Savior; everything starts and ends with You. You've been there all this time, even when I wasn't aware of your presence. I transitioned out of that season because You refused to let me stay in a low place. My life is a testament of your mercy and your grace. Thank you.

Preface

Every now and then I'm reminded of the vision I had when I was a little girl, where I saw myself observing myself. It's as if my spirit was floating in the air and observing my body. It gave me a sense of awareness that I was being assessed on how I conducted myself in this human body. This reminder usually comes at a crucial time, especially when a major decision has to be made.

It was this reminder that cultivated my accounting perspective. It created a desire to be more intentional about recording certain events or experiences that took place within my sphere of influence. One of these experiences included transitioning; whether relationally or geographically.

This led to what you now have in your hand, The Art of Transition. My objective with this book is to impart insight on:

1. How to prepare for adversity.

2. How to endure long-suffering until it's time to transition.

3. How to create and implement a strategy that will enable you to transition well - not just an escape plan, but a systematic way of guarding your mind.

My prayer is that every word you read will ignite you; like a match I hope that it strikes you in the depth of your spirit and cause a fire to be set ablaze on the inside of you so that you not just transition; but transition well. So that you can be empowered to keep growing, keep fighting and keep soaring. My prayer is that you will understand the mystery of how to keep your heart pure and remain productive in a hard season.

Content

Foreword	iii
Dedication	v
Acknowledgement	vii
Preface	xi
Necessary Roughness	1
The Assembly Line of Affliction	11
Acceptance	21
Abishag	25
Ride It Out	31
Naomi	37
Joseph	47
Think Transition	54
Ruth [ann]	61
The Art of Transition	68

'1'

Necessary Roughness

Consider it wholly joyful, my brethren, whenever you are enveloped in or encounter trials of any sort or fall into various temptations. Be assured and understand that the trial and proving of your faith bring out endurance and steadfastness and patience.
– James 1:2-3 AMP

There's only so much and no more one can do with for example the numbers five and three; while the numbers remain the same, the outcome of the equation is determined by what lies between them. In the same way, the outcome of a person's life is highly affected by what lies between their ears.

Why is it that each ear points in a different direction yet the things that lie between them point straight ahead? Why two eyes? Because, while everyone experiences transition, not everyone transition's well. In order to transition well, it's going to require twice the effort to see beyond where we're at, twice the visual ability. This means that we need both foresight and insight; foresight to see the challenge or obstacle from a distance and insight so we can understand both its necessity and how to navigate through it.

These challenges are what I call; 'necessary roughness'. They're the subtractions and divisions that affect the overall outcome of our lives; the losses and the conflicts that push us beyond our limits, and the pressure that God applies to us so that our muscles can grow.

> According to Oxford Languages, *'necessary'* is defined as being "required to be done, achieved, or present; needed; essential, determined, existing, or happening by natural laws or predestination; inevitable. According to the Cambridge Dictionary, *'roughness'* is defined as a quality of a place that is not pleasant because a lot of violent things happen there.

In other words, challenges are inevitable. Over the years, challenge after challenge has brought me to the conclusion that everything that happens to a child of God is all in His design. This conclusion doesn't deflect or reduce the intensity of the challenges, instead it amplifies my awareness and forces me to put measures in place to deal with them as they arise. So how do

we accomplish that? Well, according to James, it doesn't matter what the obstacle is, or how severe the trial may be, we should be glad, not because of the trial but because of the intended outcome.

How to prepare for adversity

So how do we prepare to endure the rough seasons of our lives? We have to start with the end in mind; therefore, we have to: B.O.M.D.A.S

- **B – Believe** that God is a good teacher. Good teachers in the natural ensure that their students are given the right tools or materials needed to be successful.

How? I'll give you two examples:
- <u>Through His Word</u> – this is why we take notes when a sermon is being preached or record prophetic words because they're not just words of

encouragement, they're also vital instructions.

- <u>Prompting us to fast, pray, re-route or reconsider a decision</u> – I will never forget the morning the police surrounded our house; their intention was to kill my brother, but they're plan was aborted because my mother got up early that morning and prayed. She always prayed for us, but that morning was unusual. For some of us it may not be as severe, it may be the prompt that prevents us from making a bad business deal or marrying the wrong person.

- **O** – Make an internal decision to **Obey** the word of God, no matter what.
- **M** – **Multiply** our efforts to remain in a place of gratitude.
- **D** – **Rightly divide** the word of truth, in that we spend time studying the

word of God so that we can know what it says about our situations. This is what gives us insight.

- **A** – Now that we know what the Word of God says, we have to then **Apply** it to our lives.

- **S** – **Subtract** all the distractions and whatever lies the enemy will try to tell us.

Every chapter of our lives has its own prerequisites in order for us to matriculate to the next chapter or phase. Even if we lose our place or footing, we're not going to be in Lodebar forever, we're in transition. As long as the earth revolves, the seasons of our life will forever be changing. I want to reinforce this definition until it becomes our default. Could it be that our life's trial is simply an explanation?

'Explanation', what is that? Think about a mathematical equation that gives the product, but we have to find what 'X' is. The teacher doesn't know how well we've comprehended the lesson until he or she gives us an opportunity to share our understanding of what was communicated. Our explanation will determine our next step; we decide whether or not that lesson has to be reiterated.

Ok, let's talk about me:
I used to be extremely tardy and it didn't bother me at all. I wasn't willing to get up earlier so that I could get to my destination on time. God in his sovereignty, knew that even though I had good intentions and met my deadlines, I still did not meet all the requirements necessary for where He would take me.

He had to give me a tutor in the form of my ex-husband, who just so happened to be active-duty military and very punctual. I quickly learned that on-time meant that I needed to be at my destination fifteen minutes before the required arrival time, while early meant, thirty

minutes prior to the arrival time. Our first argument was due my tardiness and the magnitude of it left me so traumatized that I had no choice but to learn how to be on time. It was humiliating and painful but necessary. I didn't know at that time, that 2 years later we would be relocating (transitioning) to a city where in order for me to get to work on time, I'd have to get up at least three or four hours before work begins. In that season of my life, I had to get up early enough to prepare breakfast, lunch and dinner, take the dog out and commute almost two hours for work.

It was the pre-requisite and once I explained through my behavior that I had comprehended the lesson, God started giving me favor with my co-workers and they would offer me a ride, sometimes all the way home.

I said that to say this; the hostility in the marriage worked to my advantage, it was 'necessary roughness'. So, as you continue through life's transitions, be encouraged,

challenge yourself to see every obstacle as a necessity, it's not designed to destroy you but to make you better.

Declaration

Take a deep breath and say, "Father, I may not understand what you're doing, but I'm declaring that I'm going to be just fine. It's difficult and painful but I understand that the trial and proving of my faith is only going to bring out endurance and steadfastness and patience in my life. In Jesus' name. Amen.

'2'

The Assembly Line of Affliction

'We look away from the natural realm and we focus our attention and expectation onto Jesus who birthed faith within us and who leads us forward into faith's perfection. His example is this: Because his heart was focused on the joy of knowing that you would be his, he endured the agony of the cross and conquered its humiliation, and now sits exalted at the right hand of the throne of God!'
– Hebrews 12:2 TPT

How do we look away and not allow what we see to constrict or paralyze us? Our ability to look away from the challenges we encounter in the natural realm is predicated on our level of understanding. Therefore, understanding is crucial, and the one who gives understanding has granted us full access. Like a teacher in a classroom, He leads us by giving us instructions. When we understand that we'll never have to sit an exam for a lesson we've never been taught, our faith increases. When we understand that there's a reward at the end of every obstacle, our confidence increases. Our understanding is what disciplines our eyes.

In Hebrews 2:2, "he birthed faith within us and leads us forward", could imply that before we sit in the chair to do the exam, he's already given us the answer and as we read the question, he's helping us to choose the appropriate answer. Hopefully, we would've been paying attention or didn't miss the lesson all together by skipping the class.

For example:

You know how we used to skip classes, show up late, or just not pay attention. Well, the teacher [Holy Spirit] knows that the end of semester [season] exam is scheduled for March 4th and the school or principal [Heaven or God] has already decided what topics the exam will cover.

With that in mind, the objective was to create a lesson plan that covers all the material the students would need to learn in order for them to successfully complete their exams. Unfortunately, absence, tardiness and being distracted sometimes rob us of our ability to pass the exams of life.

Most if not all of us are familiar with taking exams, it's a part of the academic system we subject ourselves and our children to, in order to advance socially. But where did this system of advancement originate from and how does it work?

At the high school I attended, we had to do several exams throughout the year which included five major exams for each subject. Each exam had at least two parts; multiple choice and written, each part was scheduled on a different day, then our overall average would determine whether or not we could advance to the next stage for that particular subject. Sometimes we did extremely well on one part of the exam and poorly on the other.

In the same way, the challenges we experience could be considered as exams, the subject could be kindness, patience, humility or self-control. The first part of the humility exam could've tested our ability to do the task we felt were beneath us, while the second part could've assessed how we conducted ourselves when we found out we were right. What if we were humble enough to do the uncomfortable task but lost a few points when we insisted on proving ourselves to be right.

The beauty about it is that God in his sovereignty, gives us an opportunity to do the test again. A good teacher doesn't allow us to matriculate to the next class until we've successfully completed the class we're in. This process of learning and testing is what I call the assembly line of affliction.

Now that we understand that the obstacles are necessary for our development, let's look at how we navigate through them.

What is an Assembly Line?

According to Investopedia, "an assembly line is a production process that breaks the manufacture of a good into steps that are completed in a pre-defined sequence. Assembly lines are the most commonly used method in the mass production of products. They reduce labor costs because unskilled workers are trained to perform specific tasks."

If we are going to transition well, we have to learn how to ask the right questions. Transitioning well demands a shift in our perspective in that it's no longer "why me Lord?" but "what are you trying to produce in me, through me or from me?" Several students take a biology class and sit the exam, but not all become a biologist, some become doctors and not all doctors are the same. Not all accounting students become accountants, some become teachers, some become cashiers, but God wants maximum productivity.

When man sees one trial after another and feels that before they could catch their breath here goes another problem; God sees a whole production process, with every trial, every obstacle being another step. Some sections of the assembly line require more pressure and takes more time, which is why some trials seem more rigorous and endless but it's all a part of the assembly line.

TRANSITION

How do you know when you've mastered a step? That answer shows up in your ability to produce. The Bible shows us how Joseph endured the process and experienced maximum productivity at every step. When we first heard about his dream, we didn't know that God was trying to produce not just a dream interpreter or household manager, in fact, Joseph advanced to becoming what I consider a chief advisor, a governmental strategist and secured the future of a whole nation.

> *"And the second he called Ephraim [to be fruitful], For [he said] God has caused me to be fruitful in the land of my affliction."*
> – Genesis 41:52 AMPC

He named his second son Ephraim (Double Prosperity), saying, "God

has prospered me in the land of my sorrow."
– Genesis 41:52 MSG

The rejection, the betrayal, the false accusation, and even the people who forgot how he helped them was all a part of the God's assembly line and at the end of it, not only was an entire nation preserved, but his ability to endure was recorded in history and we're still learning from him today.

Reflection:
Before the night ends, as you lay your head on your pillow, this time I want you to think about the fact that you're still breathing. This time I want you to wipe your tears and ask the Lord this question, "what are you trying to produce in me?" For the parent whose child has spiraled out of control; stop crying, take a deep breath and ask Him, "what are you trying to produce in this

child? What did the enemy see in my daughter or my son that threatens him? What do you want me to do about it?

Declaration

Father in the name of Jesus, I stand on your Word and I declare that the afflictions in my live are causing me to increase. Increase in fervor, increase in patience, increase in humility. I choose to look away from every distraction and fix my eyes on you Jesus as you continue to lead me forward. I will not get up from this chair, I won't quit until I've completed this test. Amen.

'3'

Acceptance

But let endurance and steadfastness and patience have full play and do a thorough work, so that you may be [people] perfectly and fully developed [with no defects], lacking in nothing.
– James 1:4 AMPC

Let the records show that we've counted the cost and we've decided to take a calculated risk on Jesus. We did the math and realized that: Disappointment + Delay = Positioning and Protection.

Let the enemy know:
- We don't know what you heard about us, but if you thought we were going to have a nervous breakdown, you were misinformed.
- if you thought we were going to give up on our children, you missed it.
- If you thought we were going to bite the bait of offense and flutter ourselves out of position, you misidentified us; because in this sense, we're not fishes, we're sheep, and this flock follows the voice of the Lord and not the voice of a stranger.

We accept the challenge. Like Peter we've decided to step out on faith because we have the

assurance that even if we fall, the Lord won't allow us to drown, He's right there with us.

Declaration

Father in the name of Jesus, I stand on your Word and I declare that you are with me. I will not run away from this thing because you are with me. Like the three Hebrew boys, you are with me in the fire. You're with me in the storm and as long as I stay on the ship my life will be preserved. Amen.

'4'

Abishag

- The Virgin Dilemma -

The girl was very beautiful; and she became the king's nurse and served him, but the king was not intimate with her.
– 1 Kings 1:4 AMP

The word of God gives us a plethora of men and women who endured difficulties and came out successful. In my opinion, Abishag was one of them. Her name was only mentioned five times, and to be honest, when you look at the challenges some of the prophets of old endured, her story seems a bit insignificant. But I wanted to bring it to our attention, so we could see an example of what could potentially be considered as suffering in silence. It's the kind of processing that one can only see with discerning eyes.

Have you ever been completely baffled? Just thrown a curve ball, felt unprepared, thought you just walked into a scheme, a trap? Have you ever felt like you just got deceived? What happens when you answer the call but the information on the other end is NOT what you had in mind?

When did beauty become a prerequisite for a nursing job? We did the math and the equation isn't adding up. What do you mean by, keep him warm? Warm how? Warm why? Couldn't they have built a fireplace to keep him warm? What about the other wives and concubines, couldn't they keep Him warm? Even though these questions could seem reasonable in today's society, the reality is that those thoughts may have never crossed Abishag's mind because at that time, being selected to serve the king in any capacity was a tremendous honor. However, while others saw the prestige that would come from being in the presence of the king only Abishag knew the cost.

It was a hard price to pay. The other women got to have children, they got to feel the comfort of a man's embrace but He wasn't able to do that for her. Willing to keep him warm, hoping that she would be the fire that ignited the king again, but her fire wasn't enough. It wasn't enough to change what was already predetermined. She had to accept it gracefully.

Let's deal with the disappointment that comes with acceptance, let's revisit the operative word we may have overlooked when the decree was made, or the instructions were given. The fine print. She accepted the call, but she had no idea that it would cost her the joy of being a mother. We know she must've handled it well because when the king's son, Adonijah, tried to use her to overthrow King Solomon, we didn't see where she was a part of the conspiracy. If she didn't handle it well, it would've been the perfect opportunity to get what the king himself couldn't give her. What did Abishag know that prevented her from becoming bitter, what was her thought process?

According to the Strong's definition, Abishag's name is translated as father of error (i.e. blundering) and the Oxford language dictionary defines 'blundering' as making or characterized by stupid or careless mistakes; clumsy.

Have you ever made a mistake and felt like it cost you everything? Maybe you've suffered as a

result of someone else's mistake? Clearly, they made a mistake because their plan didn't work.

Did they make a mistake, or was it God using the foolish things of this world to confound the wise? Literally. What would've happened had he not sustained David's life until it was Solomon's time? We know that the throne was being threatened because we saw what Adonijah did while His father was still alive. They may have made a mistake, but God had a strategy and Adonijah, consumed by envy, made a mistake in asking to marry Abishag. A mistake that cost him his life.

She was what I'd consider the celibate wife. Yes, she didn't get to experience the grandeur of affection, nor the fairy tale the other wives would've experienced while David was in the prime of his life. She didn't get to experience the joy of being a mother but what she did earned her a place in history. Graced to execute a strategy that had a dual impact.

Declaration

Father in the name of Jesus, I stand on your Word and I declare that even your seemingly foolish plans are wiser than any human plan. So even though I may not understand how this season of my life will come together, I trust your timing and your method.

I know [with great confidence] that God [who is deeply concerned about his people] causes all things to work together [as a plan] for good for those who love Him, to those who are called according to His plan and purpose. Therefore, even the foolishness I may have to deal with in this season is working together for my good. Amen.

'5'

Ride It Out

I can do all things [which He has called me to do] through Him who strengthens and empowers me [to fulfill His purpose—I am self-sufficient in Christ's sufficiency; I am ready for anything and equal to anything through Him who infuses me with inner strength and confident peace.]
– Philippians 4:13 AMP

Do you remember the silent prayer you murmured under your breath when you heard about your friend's marriage or children? Or what you vowed in your heart when that person died? Praying that you'd never have to go through that, but shortly after, it shows up at your door and now you have to deal with it, days turn to weeks, weeks turn to months, then months turn to years and you're still dealing with it. Still recovering from the tragedy, still healing, still enduring.

At this point you've become content in that you've accepted the challenges that were thrown at you and learnt to live humbly regardless of your circumstances. But what happens when contentment becomes passivity? What happens when it's not that you're content? In fact, you've only lowered your expectations so you wouldn't be disappointed. The truth is, sometimes we don't want to admit that we don't believe that there's an end to the storm we may be facing. So,

we pretend to be content, when internally, we're weak and we don't think we're going to make it.

Thankfully, we don't have to barely survive the storms, because just like Paul, we have the enabling power to do everything God has assigned for us to do. He gave Paul the strength to endure lack so much so that Paul was hungry yet happy. While he was learning how to endure, God was waiting for the right opportunity to send the Philippians to bless him.

> *"Then the sailors tried to abandon the ship; they lowered the lifeboat as though they were going to put out anchors from the front of the ship. But Paul said to the commanding officer and the soldiers, "You will all die unless the sailors stay aboard.""*
> – Acts 27:30-31 NLT

Paul is another example of what it looks like to endure until it's time to transition. So even though, at times we may feel exhausted or overwhelmed, we have to keep going. We have to ride it out like our lives depend on it.

You know as children we used to ask our mother, "is this the year God is going to bless us?" Every year, we asked the same question. We would get hit, one storm after another, but somehow, even when we had no food, we looked forward to going home because peace was there waiting for us. Months became years, but one day the Lord gave someone an opportunity to bless us, and it changed our lives. It's not that no one was concerned about us; God was simply waiting and ordering every steps to give the right person the opportunity.

If you get nothing from this book, I trust that as you read this fifth chapter, you'll tap into God's limitless enabling power called Grace; His sufficient grace. I trust that the eyes of your understanding will be opened so that you can see that God has already empowered you to withstand every storm you'll ever have to go through. You have what it takes to walk out of this season of your life with peace and not in pieces.

Take a deep breath.

Declaration

    Father in the name of Jesus, I stand on your Word and I declare I can do all things through Christ. I will not faint because you have proven that you are my strength, and you will continue to strengthen me through any test, storm or obstacle I encounter. I will NOT allow my mind to succumb to anxiety because you've given me peace. I am confident that you have already equipped me for what lies ahead, so with this assurance I am ready to 'Ride it Out'. Amen.

'6'

Naomi

Would you therefore wait till they were grown? Would you therefore refrain from marrying? No, my daughters; it is far more bitter for me than for you that the hand of the Lord is gone out against me.
– Ruth 1:13 AMPC

Promise me that when you come out of this, you won't be bitter. Promise me you won't let the test rename you, nor the storm define you. I found out that bitterness robs us of our ability to experience maximum productivity. It warps our perspective and cause us to miss opportunities. Bitterness is deceptive, it's like driving with a broken mirror. It's dangerous.

Caribbean children grow up hearing about hurricanes, it's apart of our curriculum. Every year, we brace ourselves to face the six-month hurricane season. I will never forget the trees dancing in the rain, it was scary yet intriguing. I'll never forget standing on the balcony with my siblings as my Dad examined the roof or what we called the "house top". While we were intrigued, some were terrified. The reality is that many people lost their homes and some even lost loved ones.

I noticed something as the years went by; every year there was always someone on the news or on the streets, taking us down memory lane; reminding us of everything they would've lost in the storms they would've encountered over the years. They'd complain about the help they didn't get and what the government didn't do. They forgot that the storm only lasted less than six months, they forgot the many times the storm passed over us and that even though the damage was severe it would've been far greater if God didn't divinely intervene and preserve their life.

Does that sound familiar? Of course it does, we do it too often. Like Naomi, we forget that even though we may have lost what seems to be "everything" we still had something left.

For Naomi, maybe her husband should've never left, but God allowed him leaving to work together for their good in the end. If they didn't leave Bethlehem, she would've never lost her husband and her sons, then Ruth would've never married Boaz

And she said to them, Call me not Naomi [pleasant]; call me Mara [bitter], for the Almighty has dealt very bitterly with me. I went out full, but the Lord has brought me home again empty. Why call me Naomi, since the Lord has testified against me, and the Almighty has afflicted me?'
– Ruth 1:20-21 APMC

What is bitterness?

According to the Collins dictionary, if someone is bitter after a disappointing experience or after being treated unfairly, they continue to feel angry about it.

Ok, let's talk about me:

As I sit here writing this book, trying my best to communicate His heart concerning the matter, the question that comes to mind is: how do I tell someone whose been violated not to get bitter, not to remain in that place? The reality is that bitterness is a snare, it's a trap, it's a huge pot-hole in the middle of the street that if you pay attention, you may just see it from a distance and try to avoid it. This is me showing you the result of falling in that pothole or being ensnared in that trap so that with this example you're able to identify them and not fall into them. It's from a distance because your road may be smooth and clear right now, and some of us tend to get distracted when the road is clear, that's why we use our phones while driving.

A few years ago, I decided that I didn't want to spend over than $20.00 dollars on this particular day to get my eyebrows done near the train station. I wanted to go 5mins from the house where I could get it for $7.00. Unfortunately, I stormed out of the house upset about the fact that I couldn't get a ride to the salon. In my anger, I decided to walk on the main road to the salon and guest what? That was the day I almost got kidnapped by a man who pulled up to me on the side of the street and offered me water. When I said no, he followed me all the way to my destination. Sadly, by the time I got to the salon I was so traumatized that I wasn't able to maintain my composure. The salon owners saw me crying with my nose running and refused to serve me, because they assumed that I had Covid.

Angry is an understatement for how I felt that day. I blamed the pervert for trailing me, the salon owner for not helping me and most of all; that ungrateful "roommate" for not giving me a ride. I was too bitter to see myself and how ridiculous that decision was. Until one day the Holy Spirit asked me if that's all my time was worth, if that's all I thought I was worth, He challenged me. He showed me that the husband wasn't the problem, it was an opportunity to see what was in me.

Naomi said, "he brought me home again empty. . . He testified against me" which meant that she wasn't convinced of God's sovereignty and His goodness. That it's not like God to leave us with nothing, He didn't leave the widow with nothing, she still had a flask of oil. He didn't leave Naomi with nothing, she still had Ruth. I don't care what you've lost, what the enemy has stolen from you. You may have lost your innocence, your identity or your sanity, but let me remind you that you still have something left.

She didn't lose everything; she didn't become completely hopeless. She still had the wisdom to guide her daughter-in-law so that Ruth could end up being married again. She didn't completely give up, otherwise she would've told Ruth to just remain a widow, because what's the point of loving again if they'll just end up dying and leaving you.

My question is, what do you see? Naomi saw tragedy, but God saw an opportunity.

Declaration

Father in the name of Jesus, I stand on your Word and I declare you are Jehovah Raphah, the One who heals. You not only heal diseases; you also heal mental and emotional wounds. With this assurance I ask you to heal me from every disappointment and anything that was said or done to me that left a mark on my soul.

I know that words are like graffiti on a wall, so I don't want to mask the negative words, instead I want you to erase it completely with the water of your word. Rewrite your words on the tablets of my heart instead of what was said. Cause me to remember your goodness instead of the things that disappointed me. Give me an eternal perspective so I won't be offended when I'm faced with challenges.

Heal me completely so that when the enemy comes looking for bitterness, resentment and unforgiveness, he won't find those things in me. Today I choose to forgive, because I understand that it will be like a vaccine that fortifies my spiritual immune system against bitterness and unforgiveness. Amen.

'7'

Joseph

"The Lord was with Joseph, and he [even though a slave] became a successful and prosperous man; and he was in the house of his master, the Egyptian."
– Genesis 39:2 AMP

The truth is, we get to read the stories in the Bible after knowing how they would end, but did the children of Israel know that the reason why God led them through the wilderness was so that they could learn how to fight? I guess by now they should've known that He wasn't going to set them up to fail.

What about Joseph, did He know that God was going to send him to Egypt as a slave? Was he there when the request was made:

"I need someone to take Joseph to Egypt. . . first we'll l have to get rid of his coat." Who signed off on chains? Did they not hear about the dreams he had? How dare they?! Thankfully, according to Genesis 39, "even though he was a slave, the Lord was with him and he became prosperous and successful".

Seven more years before Rachel could marry Jacob, then six sons of Leah later, Rachel finally had Joseph. It seems as if she was always waiting on Leah.

> *"This time my husband will honor me with gifts—I've given him six sons!" She named him Zebulun (Honor). Last of all she had a daughter and named her Dinah. And then God remembered Rachel. God listened to her and opened her womb. She became pregnant and had a son. She said, "God has taken away my humiliation." She named him Joseph (Add), praying, "May God add yet another son to me."*
> – Genesis 30:20-24 MSG

Fast forward, Joseph got a seven year strategic plan. Could it be that the reason why Joseph was able to comprehend and execute the strategy God gave him, was because the number seven, famine and suffering wasn't strange to him? Did his mother tell him how his dad had to work seven more years before he could marry her? Did he observe that he was the seventh son for his father? Did he remember that it was after he was born that his father asked to leave Laban (his grandfather) and that's when God gave him a strategy? Did he observe his father's life and learned the voice of God and the mind of God by how his father lived? So that years, he would be the one to hear the mind of God for the famine? Where did he learn how to exchange food for livestock and food for labor? Did he remember how his father worked for Laban for his mother and another season with livestock as his wages? How is it that a seventeen year old had the maturity and the staying power to endure the trauma of being raised without a mother, rejected by his brothers, no longer with his father and still thrive in prison? What did Joseph learn in the background? When did he move from just dreaming to now interpreting dreams?

> *"But don't be upset, and don't be angry with yourselves for selling me to this place. It was God who sent me here ahead of you to preserve your lives."*
> – Genesis 45:5 NLT

He came to this conclusion at the end of the affliction but because these things were written for us as examples, we now have foresight. We get to live with an understanding that the God who enabled Joseph to prosper and become successful in the midst of tragedy, is the same God orchestrating our lives and He's given us the same ability. Maybe it's not about us; have we considered those lives who will be affected by the end result of the season we're in?

Laban said "the Lord has blessed me because of you;

> *"But Laban said to him, 'If I have found favor in your sight, stay with me; for I have learned [from the omens in divination and by experience] that the Lord has blessed me because of you.'"*
> – Genesis 30:27 AMP

Jacob was working like a slave, but Laban wasn't the only beneficiary; Joseph benefited from what He saw His father do.

Declaration

Father in the name of Jesus, I stand on your Word and I declare that even in the most difficult season of my life, you are with me. You're giving me the wisdom and the strategy to prosper and to be successful despite the oppositions. Thank you for clarity and understanding. In Jesus' name. Amen.

'8'

Think Transition

"Now Joseph dreamed a dream, and he told it to his brothers, and they hated him even more...His brothers said to him, Are you actually going to reign over us? Are you really going to rule and govern us as your subjects?" So they hated him even more for [telling them about] his dreams and for his [arrogant] words."
– Genesis 37:5,8 AMP

TRANSITION

The Joseph perspective came Saturday night before I went to bed. He said, "use Joseph". At first I was a bit apprehensive, I didn't understand how my story and what I intended to share related to Joseph. So He told me to go and read it until I saw it.

I started from chapter 37 and when I got to chapter 39, that's when he unveiled the mystery of how my life related to the Joseph's story.

People may ask:
- Why did you stay?
- Why didn't you jump in front of the train?

My simple answer would be: "because that's not what I saw"

> *". . . For I am God, and there is no one else; I am God, and there is no one like Me, Declaring the end and the result from the beginning, And from ancient times the things*

which have not [yet] been done, Saying, 'My purpose will be established, And I will do all that pleases Me and fulfills My purpose."
– Isaiah 46:9-10 AMP

I didn't jump in front of the train because I didn't see the vision come to pass yet. I didn't understand how I would get from walking home in the cold to being free, but I knew that He promised me something and I needed to live long enough to see it. That's not what I saw. I was determined not to walk away empty handed, even if the only thing I had left was my dignity, I didn't want to be ashamed of the woman I had become.

Joseph had a vision; Jeremiah had a word and Jesus had a promise. I realized that in order for us to endure the suffering for however long it takes, it's going to require us to make some hard

decisions. First, we have to decide to cross over and secondly, we have to decide what lines we'll never cross. Joseph had to make a decision not to succumb to Potiphar's wife when she insisted on him laying with her. No one was there, he could've easily got away with it, or so it seems. Jesus had to decide not to succumb to the enemy's temptations. It's the dividing line between transitioning well and sitting the test again. It's the line between victory and tragedy, because for some of us, our lives are depending on us treading lightly.

So tread lightly, a disease may be waiting on the other side, tread lightly. People's lives are depending on you, tread lightly. For Israel, a whole generation died in the wilderness because they didn't transition well. There's glory at the end of this season, tread lightly. It won't always be like this, tread lightly.

I need you to make a decision today. Decide that you're not going to succumb to the pressure, that even on broken pieces, you're going to come out of this with your dignity.

Declaration

Father in the name of Jesus, I stand on your Word and I declare that you are God, and there is no one like You;
- Before I even entered this season
- Before I started this assignment or this ministry
- Before I got this job
- Before I had these children
- Before I entered this marriage/relationship

. . .you've already determined the outcome and you're already aware of the challenges assigned to it. Even though the enemy is trying to interfere; God let your purpose be established. I offer no resistance; do whatever pleases You and fulfill Your purpose in this season, with this assignment, at this job, with these children and in this marriage in Jesus name. Amen.

'9'

Ruth [ann]

"My troubles turned out all for the best— they forced me to learn from your textbook. Truth from your mouth means more to me than striking it rich in a gold mine."
– Psalms 119:72 MSG

"My suffering was good for me, for it taught me to pay attention to your decrees."
– Psalms 119:71 NLT

Transition

The Vow

"To my husband,

"Wherefore his servants said unto him, Let there be sought for my lord the king a young virgin: and let her stand before the king, and let her cherish him, and let her lie in thy bosom, that my lord the king may get heat." - 1 Kings 1:2

At the appointed time He sent for me, like Esther He called me away from my country to serve a king. I am your gift, your treasure, your prize. You are my unspoken request, my heart's desire. In my weakness you covered me, in my brokenness you didn't look at me through carnal eyes. Let me lie in your bosom and minister to you. May my words be nourishment to your soul. I'm here to honor and to cherish you. Today as we become one flesh, I pray that the fire inside of me will ignite you and propel you further into your destiny.

Like Abishag to her king, here I am your majesty."

She was Abishag, deprived of affection and attention, the celibate wife, wrestling with rejection. She was married three months short of five years; I guess the marriage didn't make it to grace. She used to cry when she remembered her vows.

To some she was the wife, but to him she was just Molly the maid. Making a bed she wasn't allowed to sleep in, but it wasn't about her ability to arouse him. It was about her ability to serve and still maintain her integrity whether or not he responded favorably.

She didn't even understand the depth of what she had declared over her own life when she made that vow on her wedding day. It wasn't a coincidence that she was relegated to just being the help; she had insisted on taking a chance that to some didn't make any sense so, God in His sovereignty capitalized on the opportunity to both refine and prepare her. What she perceived as rejection was His divine protection. Having accepted his flaws, she had made an inner vow that nothing he did would make her love him any less.

Now her words were being tried. Tried by every insult, by every neglect. Every time she was deprived, mishandled or disrespected it was her words being tried. She didn't walk out of it, she didn't find his replacement even though she was given permission to; instead like Naomi, she became bitter.

Yes, she was Naomi, heartbroken and disappointed. She felt like it took everything; her sanity, her identity, her value, after all, she gave him her virginity; it was the main thing she thought made her valuable. She felt a bitterness that made her heart race when he entered the room. Even the very sound of his voice made her tremble. She became too bitter to realize how God was sustaining her, how he was training her. She learned to design a website using wix, published her first financial blog, designed one of her business logos and so much more in that season. Can you imagine the things she would've

been able to produce if she did not allow her heart to be poisoned with BITTERNESS? Understand that the serpent is waiting to wrap himself around us and suck the life out of us; that's what bitterness does, it stifles! So while we are going through our transition, we have to become resolute in our mind and in our spirit that we will not become bitter. We will not change our names by allowing our situation to define us. She didn't lose everything. She didn't loose her dignity nor her tenacity.

She was Joseph, the tragedy was God's transportation. Overtime, she learned that there was no need to take it personal, because it was the tool that developed the strategist in her as she sat in her room night after night planning and crying. The affliction was designed to cultivate the Joseph inside of her, to make her a solutionist. Joseph said, "I am Joseph" – in the same way, at the end of the trial she was still the dreamer. What it did was add another dimension to her life, gave the soldier in her

some stripes and made her realize that lions see clear in the dark.

By the way, I'm her. Just incase you haven't figured it out; my name is Ruthann Christiane Johnson. I sat the test, and the results are in:

The Lord gives and the Lord takes away, blessed be the name of the Lord. He gave me what I thought I wanted, and the Lord took it away. There's no need to feel condemned about it ending, he didn't put me out, this was the Lord's doing and now I can say that it was good that I was afflicted, because the affliction:

> **I learned**
> - how to bear up under pressure
> - how to know the voice of God
> - how to plan more effectively
> - how to design even better.
> - that I wasn't as loving, forgiving, humble and submissive as I should be.
> - that the rejection I felt was God's protection.
> - that His Grace was and still is sufficient not just to endure but to transition well. Afterall, Ann means "grace."

- dealt with the pride in my soul and the need for validation.
- it confronted the insubordination.

- it identified every dysfunction and every defect.
- it helped me find my true value.
- it showed me, my propensity to be bitter and unforgiving.
- it confronted the inconsistency.
- it unlocked gifts in me I didn't even know I had.
- it made me eat healthier.

It taught me:
- how to love, how to sacrifice and how to endure. How to be wise, discerning, strategic, discipline and more sociable.
- when to speak and when to keep silent.

The records have solidified the fact that those seasons were divinely orchestrated to bring me into my place of destiny. Therefore, it was good that I was afflicted.

'10'

The Art of Transition

And then, after your brief suffering, the God of all loving grace, who has called you to share in his eternal glory in Christ, will personally and powerfully restore you and make you stronger than ever. Yes, he will set you firmly in place and build you up.
– 1 Peter 5:10 TPT

Now that you understand that this is merely a test and you see the necessity of it [the 'WHAT and WHY'], it is imperative that you transition well. Transition requires persistence, tenacity, humility, strategy and wise counsel.

Like Job, we have to come to a place where our default is thanksgiving and complete confidence and faith in God. This is what enables us to walk into every transition boldly. There is a way to transition, it's the difference between overtaking a vehicle when you can see clearly in front of you and overtaking on a curve; the latter makes absolutely no sense and could be fatal. In the same way, when we transition well, we prevent unnecessary tragedies. David transitioned from being a shepherd boy to a king, he could've killed Saul, but he chose not to. Whether it's from being single to being married, moving from one job to the next or from one ministry to another, we can transition well.

Definitions:

According to Oxford Languages, the word *'art'* is defined as a skill at doing a specified thing, typically one acquired through practice. For example, "the art of conversation".
The word *'transition'* is defined as the process or a period of changing from one state or condition to another.

The beauty about it is that even if we did not handle the last season well, we have an opportunity to do better, because transitioning well is truly a skill that we acquire through practice. If Joseph didn't transition well, he would've killed all his brothers for what they did to him, or he would've left them to suffer in the famine.

Here's my final admonition:
- Be objective – don't allow fear or anger to influence your decisions.

- Surround yourself with wise and godly counsel.
- Don't allow yourself to suffer in silence, ask for help. The Holy Spirit is your first point of contact. He'll show you where to look, who to ask and what to listen to or read to get the help you need.
- Be slow to get angry and quick to forgive.
- If you have nothing good to say, don't say anything at all – because words do have power and when they told us that sticks and stones may break your bones, but words don't do a thing to you, they lied.

Let's just settle the matter:

We don't get to choose our trials, but we've decided to transition well. We've decided to have maximum productivity. We're determined to exploit every low blow and catch every curve ball. We say, "Lord, you can trust us. We know you will never set us up to fail, that the test isn't to make us look bad, it's to reveal the treasures that are hidden inside of us. We are grateful for the opportunity to get to know you, because every test reveals a different part of your nature"

Tested for the sake of the word and having done all to stand, we're going to keep standing.

Declaration

Father in the name in the name of Jesus, I stand on your Word and I declare I can do all things through Christ. I will not faint because you are my strength. I will not crumble under the pressure because you are the one who keeps me from falling. The weight is only strengthening my muscles so that at the end of it I'll be stronger than ever. I won't worry about what I have lost because you promise to restore me. My perspective has shifted, I'm not a victim but a victor and I will transition well.

About the Author

Ruthann Johnson is a hidden gem whose life is committed to advancing the kingdom of God. She's a strategist who is constantly seeking ways of becoming more effective.

Let's Connect
AUTHOR | EDITIOR

Christiane - the Editor was designed with the upcoming author in mind. We provide editorials services for non-fiction bible-based literature, giving our clients the opportunity to get an objective assessment of their manuscript before it gets published. For more information, please email us at ruthann.c@icloud.com.

Loved reading this book?

GIVE IT AWAY!

If reading this book has impacted your life and you would like to order more copies for those in your sphere of influence (perhaps your church, small group, company, friends or family), please contact us to get a discount on a bulk order.at: ruthann.c@icloud.com.

Who needs to read this book?

Somehow you came across this book and you're trying to decipher whether or not it's worth the read. If you still cry over who betrayed, disappointed, didn't help or mishandled you; this book is for you.

If you keep rehearsing what was done, it sounds like you might be picking at a scab for a wound that hasn't been completely healed. Sometimes we rip off the scabs thinking that our wounds are healed only to find ourselves bleeding.

Some scabs or hidden while others are visible, regardless of what it is, or what bruised your soul; this book was written just for you. To help shift your perspective, to re-introduce you to the one who can truly heal you and get you right back on your feet again so you can transition through the phases of your life well.

www.ingramcontent.com/pod-product-compliance
Lightning Source LLC
Chambersburg PA
CBHW060400050426
42449CB00009B/1837